BOOK OF PRAYERS & BIBLE VERSES

JANET HUTCHFUL

Copyright © 2024 by Janet Hutchful

All rights reserved. This book or any portion thereof may not be reproduced or used in any manner whatsoever without the express written permission of the publisher except for the use of brief quotations in a book review.

Limits of Liability and Disclaimer of Warranty

The author and publisher shall not be liable for your misuse of this material. This book is strictly for informational purposes. The purpose of this book is to educate and entertain. The author and publisher do not guarantee anyone following these techniques, suggestions, tips, ideas, or strategies will become successful. The author and publisher shall have neither liability nor responsibility to anyone with respect to any loss or damage caused, or alleged to be caused, directly or indirectly by the information contained in this book. Views expressed in this publication do not necessarily reflect the views of the publisher.

Cover: Designs By Triv ilovedesignsbytriv@gmail.com

Printed in the United States of America
Keen Vision Publishing, LLC
www.publishwithkvp.com
ISBN: 979-8-9912210-7-8

For God, who instructed me to write this.
For my children, whom I love dearly.

INTRODUCTION

ABC Book of Prayers and Scriptures is a compilation of scripture and revelations God shared with me. It is intended to serve as a convenient companion to aspiring "citizens of the kingdom" who would like straight-forward reminders of basic Scriptural truths directly from the Word of God—truths that are directly applicable to the present age and time for all levels of readers. It is not intended to be a source of in-depth study, but rather a friendly and quick reminder of some "ABCs" and "123s" that can be useful on a daily basis and/or between major activities without requiring lengthy words, numbers, focus, or investment of time. The alphabetic and numeric arrangement of Biblical words and numbers is intended to help stimulate your recall of certain truths long after they have been read. May God's spirit embrace you as you read along in this book and refer to it occasionally.

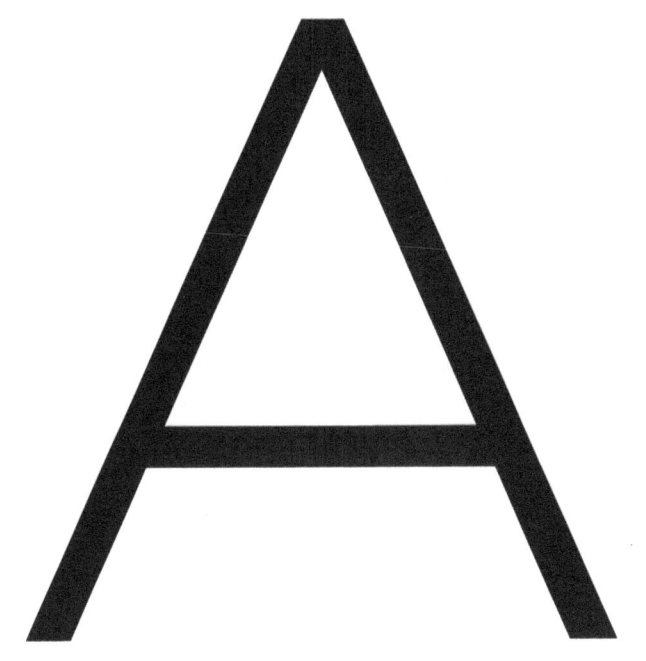

ABIDE

dwell in; stay in or take safe residence at

SCRIPTURES

Lord, who may **abide** *in your tabernacle? Who may dwell in your holy hill?*

PSALM 15:1-2

If you keep my commandments, you will **abide** *in my love, just as I have kept my Father's commandments and abide in his love.*

JOHN 15:10

HOW THE SCRIPTURES APPLY TO ME

The Tabernacle of God and the love of Jesus are safe spiritual places. There is no better place to be than in the presence and care of the most high God.

PRAYER

Lord, give me a real desire, spirit, and strength to do all that You require to abide in the safety of Your presence and love. This is my earnest prayer in Jesus' name. Amen.

BELIEVE

*trust and have no doubt;
be at rest that something is true*

SCRIPTURES

Jesus said to him, "If you can **believe,** *all things are possible to him who* **believes."**

MARK 9:23

Therefore I say to you, whatever things you ask when you pray, **believe** *that you receive them, and you will have them.*

MARK 11:24

HOW THE SCRIPTURES APPLY TO ME

Believing is the key that makes all things possible for us. Jesus encourages believers to trust in God, pray without doubting, and be assured that He is faithful to grant what we righteously ask.

PRAYER

Lord Jesus, help me believe with all my heart in You, in Your power, and in Your word, so that I can receive all right things that I ask for, as You promised to true believers. In Your name, I pray. Amen.

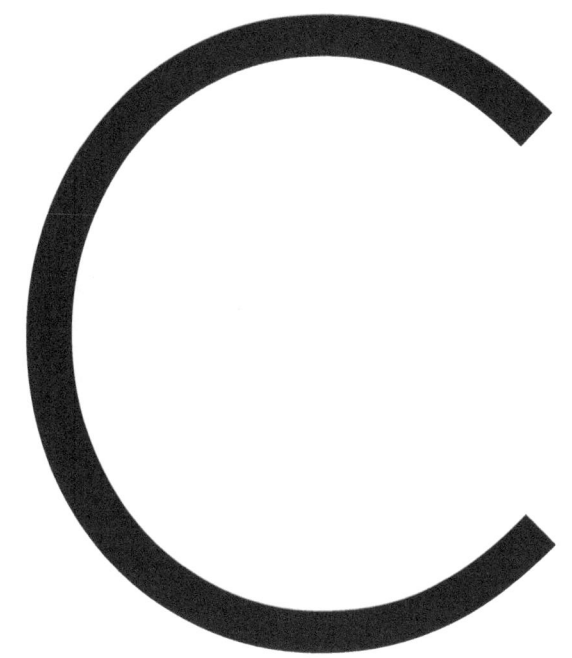

CONFESS

own up to, admit, or declare openly

SCRIPTURES

I acknowledged my sin to you, and my iniquity I have not hidden. I said, "I will **confess** *my transgressions unto the LORD," and you forgave the iniquity of my sin.*

PSALM 32:5

If we **confess** *our sins, He is faithful and just to forgive us our sins and to cleanse us from all unrighteousness.*

1 JOHN 1:9

HOW THE SCRIPTURES APPLY TO ME

We should confess our sins, whether big or small. All sin is ungodly and displeasing to God. He is willing to forgive us if we are genuinely sorry for our sins. When we humbly own up to our sin and ask God to forgive us, He will not hold our sins against us.

PRAYER

Dear heavenly Father, I have sinned and come short of pleasing You. I know that my life must please You in order to be all that You have designed me to be. I am truly sorry for all of my sins. Please forgive me. In accordance with Your word, I confess with my mouth that Jesus is Lord. Amen.

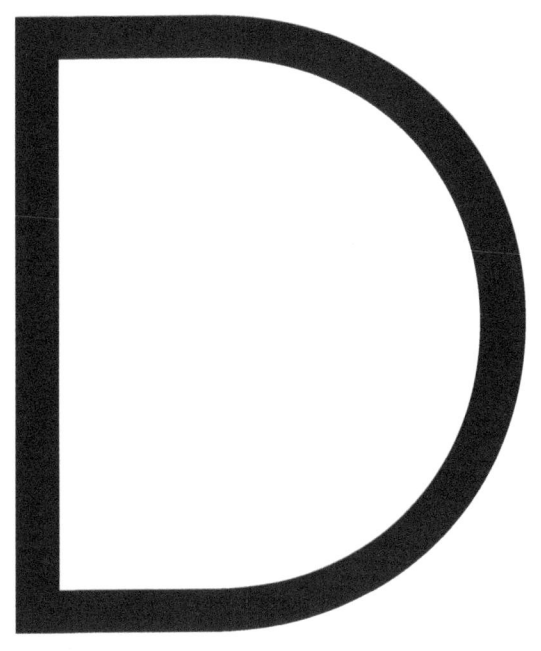

DELIVER

give over something or someone; rescue or save

SCRIPTURES

And forgive us our sins, for we also forgive everyone who is indebted to us. And do not lead us into temptation, but **deliver** *us from the evil one.*

LUKE 11:4

The Lord knows how to **deliver** *the godly out of temptations and to reserve the unjust under punishment for the day of judgment.*

2 PETER 2:9

HOW THE SCRIPTURES APPLY TO ME

From His own experience, Jesus knows how Satan brings temptations to act against the heavenly Father's will. God delivers us and teaches us how to flee from temptations by using the Scriptures.

PRAYER

Our Father in heaven, forgive me of the temptations into which I have already fallen. Deliver me from the temptations that are presented to me by evildoers. I know that I must forgive those who sin against me so that I can qualify for you to deliver me from temptations of the evil one; this I will do. In Jesus' name, I pray, Amen.

ETERNAL LIFE

the state of never experiencing death

SCRIPTURES

That whoever believes in Him should not perish but have eternal life.

JOHN 3:15

And as Moses lifted up the serpent in the wilderness, even so must the Son of Man be lifted up, that whosoever believes in Him should not perish but have **eternal life.**

JOHN 3:14-15

That whoever believes in Him should not perish but have eternal life.

ROMANS 6:23

HOW THE SCRIPTURES APPLY TO ME

God's promises eternal life for all who have given their lives to Christ in this world. We must repent of our sinful nature and come openly to Christ so that we will be covered by the blood He shed on the cross from eternal punishment.

PRAYER

Father in heaven, I believe in Your Son, Jesus Christ. I believe that He died on the cross so that His shed blood would cover me from eternal punishment for my sins. I present myself to You, in the name of Jesus Christ, to live as You would have me live and then to live with You forever in paradise. Amen.

FAITH

heartfelt assurance that what is unseen or unexperienced will certainly come to pass

SCRIPTURES

But the just shall live by his faith.

HABAKKUK 2:4B

Therefore, having been justified by faith, *we have peace with God through our Lord Jesus Christ.*

ROMANS 5:1

But without faith *it is impossible to please Him, for he who comes to God must believe that He is, and that He is a rewarder of those who diligently seek Him.*

HEBREWS 11:6

HOW THE SCRIPTURES APPLY TO ME

The key to our relationship with God the Father and Jesus Christ is our pure belief and faith in God the Father and His word through Jesus Christ. The Scripture puts it as plainly as possible that it is impossible to please God without faith.

PRAYER

Heavenly Father, in the name of Jesus, teach me by the Holy Spirit how to build my faith and please You more. I want to be more fruitful in Your service to not only reap Your rewards but to also glorify You. In Jesus' name, I pray. Amen.

GOD-THE FATHER

Creator of the heavens by His Word, Jesus, and the Holy Spirit. He created man in His own image to obey Him and rule the earth.

SCRIPTURES

In the beginning **God** *created the heaven and the earth.*

GENESIS 1:1

Then **God** *said, "Let us make man in Our image; according to Our likeness; let them have dominion over the fish of the sea, over the birds of the air, and over the cattle, over all the earth and every creeping thing that creeps on the earth."*

GENESIS 1:26

The heaven, even the heavens, are the **LORD'S**; *but the earth He has given to the children of men.*

PSALM 115:16

HOW THE SCRIPTURES APPLY TO ME

God, the Father, is the supreme maker, head, and ruler of all. He made mankind in His image and likeness to rule the earth and enjoy being in dominion as long as we obey Him.

PRAYER

Heavenly Father, I am grateful You included me as one of the children of men to whom You gave the earth. I also acknowledge the obedience You commanded of us all. Help me to be obedient to You and keep Your Word so I can enjoy the benefits You have provided and avoid the result of not obeying You. In Your name, I pray. Amen.

HOLY SPIRIT

The Spirit which proceeds from God the Father and Jesus the Word; The third person in the divine Godhead; the executor, doer, and communicator of what is spoken from the Father through the word with equal power; comforter, director, helper, operator, and teacher.

SCRIPTURES

Jesus answered, "Most assuredly, I say to you, unless one is born of water and **the spirit,** *he cannot enter the kingdom of God.*

JOHN 3:5

And I will pray the Father, and He will give you another **Helper,** *that He may abide with you forever.*

JOHN 14:16

Then Peter said to them, "Repent, and let every one of you be baptized in the name of Jesus Christ for the remission of sins; and you shall receive the gift of the **Holy Spirit.**

ACTS 2:38

HOW THE SCRIPTURES APPLY TO ME

The Holy Spirit is God's gift to all who obey the requirements given by Jesus Christ and ask for Him. He will teach and help those in whom He dwells to live a blessed and purposeful life in the spiritual kingdom of God here on earth.

PRAYER

Heavenly Father, I thank You for the opportunity You have made for me to be baptized in the Holy Spirit. I am thankful to have Him dwell within me and help me be faithful to You and receive all the benefits as a member of Your kingdom. In Jesus' name, I pray. Amen.

IMAGE OF GOD

"Likeness of God," (or pattern of the original); the design in which God created man. Jesus, while on earth, was the "express image of God" or the image of God in the highest sense.

SCRIPTURES

So God created man in His own image; in the image of God He created them.

GENESIS 1:27

who being the brightness of His glory and the express image of his person, and upholding all things by the word of His power, when He had by Himself purged our sins, sat down at the right hand of the majesty on high.

HEBREWS 1:3

HOW THE SCRIPTURES APPLY TO ME

We are all created in God's image. Jesus represents the image of God the Father in the highest sense. God the Father wants us to conform to the image of Jesus naturally and spiritually. God does not want us to create other images to give ourselves to by religion or by social custom. He is not pleased with the disfiguring of our bodies that were made in His image. Many in the world are doing so ignorantly, thinking they are making a good statement, but are really dishonoring our heavenly creator.

PRAYER

Lord, help me conform to the spiritual image of Jesus Christ and honor the body You have formed for me on earth in accordance with Your wisdom. In Your name, I pray. Amen.

JESUS

the embodied Word of God, equal in power and glory; the only name given under heaven whereby men must be saved.

SCRIPTURES

And she will bring forth a Son, and you shall call His name Jesus, for He will save His people from their sins.

MATTHEW 1:21

And behold, you will conceive in your womb and bring forth a Son, and shall call His name Jesus.

LUKE 1:31

The Spirit of the LORD is upon Me, because He has anointed Me to preach the gospel to the poor; He has sent Me to heal the broken hearted, to proclaim liberty to the captives and recovery of sight to the blind, to set at liberty those who are oppressed; to proclaim the acceptable year of the LORD.

LUKE 4:18

HOW THE SCRIPTURES APPLY TO ME

This is the age God desires the gospel of Jesus Christ to be preached, believed, and acted upon by all mankind. This is the time for mankind to be saved from the curse of inborn sin, which is spiritual death and everlasting punishment in hell.

PRAYER

Lord Jesus, I believe You are the Son of God, and You gave Your life for me so that I might be saved from everlasting death and punishment in hell. I repent for my sins and have now presented myself to You as a vessel for the Holy Spirit. Use me for your purpose in this life. Help me learn to be led by the Holy Spirit. Teach me to use the ability You have given me to continue Your anointed work. I desire to bear much good fruit that is pleasing in Your sight, that I may receive blessings and rewards on earth and everlasting life hereafter. Amen.

KINGDOM OF GOD

the existence of life in the universe under the direct supreme authority, power, and rulership of God, conditioned upon free will choice.

SCRIPTURES

Your kingdom is an everlasting kingdom, and Your dominion endures throughout all generations.

PSALM 145:13

But seek first the kingdom of God and His righteousness, and all these things shall be added to you.

MATTHEW 6:33

Jesus answered, "Most assuredly, I say to you, unless one is born of water and the Spirit, he cannot enter the kingdom of God.

JOHN 3:5

For the kingdom of God is not eating and drinking, but righteousness and peace and joy in the Holy Spirit.

ROMANS 14:17

HOW THE SCRIPTURES APPLY TO ME

Our primary interest in life should not be gathering material things that the world seeks. The aim of our lives should be to live as citizens in the kingdom of God. Jesus promises that the things the world seeks after will be added to us by God, who works all things together for the good of those who are members of His kingdom and seek to fulfill His purpose.

PRAYER

Heavenly Father, You already know all I need to live righteously and have peace and joy in the Holy Spirit. Teach me how to seek Your kingdom first and not put material things before You. I promise to use Your blessings to plant good seeds so that I can reap the benefits of both Your kingdom and my natural desires and comfort. I ask in Jesus' name that You accept this prayer and grant me favor in Your sight. Amen.

LEARNING AND KNOWLEDGE

*familiarity with truth, whether from experience,
teaching, or study*

SCRIPTURES

Take My yoke upon you and learn from Me, for I am gentle and lowly in heart, and you will find rest for your souls.
MATTHEW 11:29

It is written in the prophets, "And they shall all be taught by God." Therefore, everyone who has heard and learned from the Father comes to Me (Jesus).
JOHN 6:45

Study to show thyself approved unto God, a workman that needeth not to be ashamed, rightly dividing the word of truth.
2 TIMOTHY 2:15

HOW THE SCRIPTURES APPLY TO ME

Jesus taught that learning about Him and the salvation He brings should not be taken lightly. We should be serious about disciplining ourselves to learn and possess knowledge of the truth about Him in the manner in which farmers put a yoke upon oxen to control their working behavior. God the Father positions us to hear the gospel and come to Jesus Christ. Still, the Apostle in the Book of Timothy teaches that to be approved of God as a kingdom worker, we must study how to divide the Scriptures and be bold and not ashamed rightly.

PRAYER

Dear Father in heaven, thank You for working things for me to hear the gospel of Jesus and come unto Him for salvation. Now, I pray that You teach me by Your Holy Spirit how to study the Scriptures and be more knowledgeable of truth instead of notions and fables of the world. Teach me how to be a fruitful worker in accordance with the words of Jesus, my Savior. And it is in His name I pray. Amen.

MERCIFUL

exercising compassion and pity toward the ills of others; a characteristic of God that He wants His kingdom people to show.

SCRIPTURES

Therefore be merciful, just as your (heavenly) Father also is merciful.

LUKE 6:36

Indeed we count them blessed who endure. You have heard of the perseverance of Job and seen the end intended by the Lord—that the Lord is very compassionate and merciful.

JAMES 5:11

HOW THE SCRIPTURES APPLY TO ME

If we think back, all of us will realize that we have benefitted in some way from the merciful nature of God. Jesus taught us to be merciful to others. God will extend tender mercies and loving-kindness to us who express the same characteristics toward others.

PRAYER

Lord, I am continually thankful to You for Your loving-kindness and tender mercies toward me. Create in me the kind of compassion for others You show toward me so that I can always be qualified to receive the benefits of Your compassionate nature. In Jesus' name, so let it be. Amen.

NEW COVENANT

All who believe and confess faith in Jesus Christ are saved from everlasting punishment under the curse from Adam's sin.

SCRIPTURES

"Behold, the days are coming," says the Lord, "when I will make a new covenant with the house of Israel and the house of Judah—not according to the covenant that I made with their fathers in the day that I took them by the hand to lead them out of the land of Egypt, My covenant which they broke..."

JEREMIAH 31:31-32

Likewise He also took the cup after supper, saying, "This cup is the new covenant in My blood, which is shed for you..."

LUKE 22:20

HOW THE SCRIPTURES APPLY TO ME

The new covenant shows that God loves us and is willing to forgive each of us of our sins, but we must fulfill our part to complete the agreement and be saved. Our part is to believe in Jesus Christ and accept Him as our savior by obeying His requirement to be baptized in His Holy Spirit.

PRAYER

Lord Jesus, I confess that I am a sinner because of the sin of Adam. I now confess my belief that You shed Your precious blood and died on the cross so that I might be saved and have Your Spirit abide in me. Continue to help me live a life that is fruitful and pleasing to You. Amen.

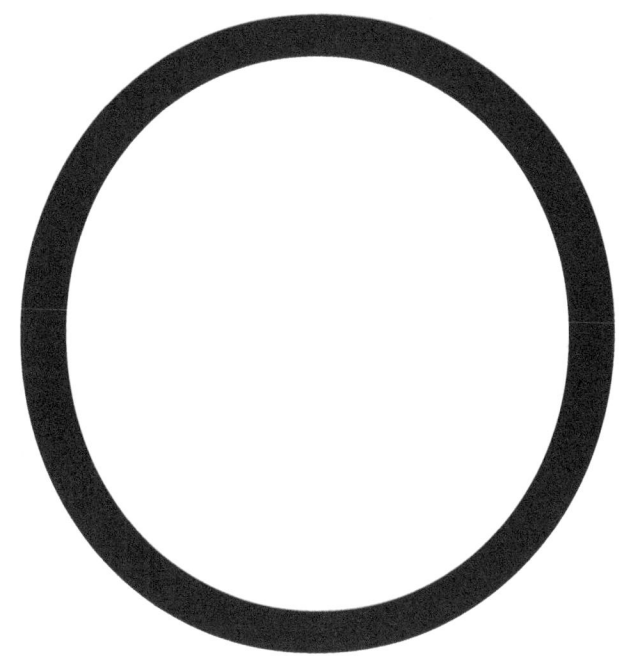

OBEDIENCE

submitting to authority; the behavior of being willing to honor and follow the commands and desires of righteous authority, the highest authority being God.

SCRIPTURES

*For as by one man's (Adam's) disobedience many were made sinners, so also by one Man's (Jesus') **obedience** many will be made righteous.*

ROMANS 5:19

*As **obedient** children, not conforming yourselves to the former lusts, as in your ignorance;*

1 PETER 1:14

HOW THE SCRIPTURES APPLY TO ME

It is God's will that we put ourselves in a position to be saved and continuously receive the blessings of His grace by hearing and obeying His voice, which comes by way of the Holy Scriptures, His Holy ministers and servants, and the Spirit He has given to all who believe and are baptized in the Spirit.

PRAYER

Lord, help me to learn the kind of obedience that pleases You so that I can qualify for all of the blessings that You have for me and be more fruitful for You. Amen.

PROMISE

a personal assurance or vow; that which has been declared will certainly be performed

SCRIPTURES

"Honor your father and mother," which is the first commandment with **promise:** *"that it may be well with you and you may live long on the earth."*

EPHESIANS 6:2-3

Blessed is the man who endures temptation; for when he has been approved, he will receive the crown of life which the Lord has **promised** *to those that love Him.*

JAMES 1:12

HOW THE SCRIPTURES APPLY TO ME

God will surely fulfill all His promises to us, those above are just a few of them. He will stand by His word. We should also be faithful and fulfill our promises to God to be partakers of His promises.

PRAYER

Lord God almighty, grant me the spirit of belief that when You make a promise, You will certainly fulfill it; also, make me understand that You make promises on Your terms and not mine. Please help me to be in a position to receive Your righteous promises. In Jesus' name, I pray. Amen.

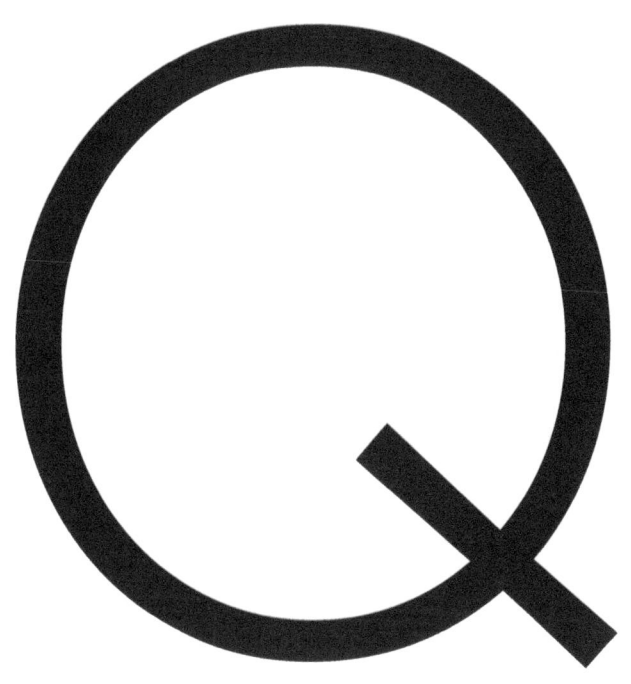

QUENCH

*to cool or make less active; to put out,
as fire or passion.*

SCRIPTURES

Do not quench the Spirit.

1 THESSALONIANS 5:19

Above all, taking the shield of faith with which you will be able to QUENCH all the fiery darts of the wicked one.

EPHESIANS 6:16

HOW THE SCRIPTURES APPLY TO ME

Do not force the cooling down of the Spirit of God. The Spirit could activate someone during church, worship service, or other settings. On the other hand, by our faith in God, His mighty power will enable us to quench or put out the fiery weapons of Satan that He throws at us by way of his wicked ones.

PRAYER

Almighty God of heaven and earth, help me always to be alert to the working of your Holy Spirit so that I will never quench the Holy Spirit in my presence or in myself. Please give me the faith in You that will shield me from the attempts of evil ones against me and put out the fire of their evil works. In Jesus' name, I pray, Amen.

RAISE

to lift to a higher level; to bring to life or activate.

SCRIPTURES

And God both RAISED up the Lord and will also raise us up by His power.

1 CORINTHIANS 6:14

Knowing that He who raised up the Lord Jesus will also raise us up with Jesus, and will present us with you.

2 CORINTHIANS 4:14

HOW THE SCRIPTURES APPLY TO ME

While Jesus was on earth, one of the acts He performed was raising people from the dead. He was crucified for our sins so that we may have everlasting life by believing He was the son of God. Just as God raised Jesus from the dead, all of us who believe that Jesus died for us will rise up to live for Him and be raised up to meet Him in the air, whether we are alive or dead, when He returns for us.

PRAYER

Jesus, precious Savior, I am thankful to you for dying for me. I am grateful to God the Father for raising you up so that I may rise up also and spend eternity in heaven instead of in everlasting punishment, bearing the curse of Adam's sin. I thank You, Father God, for raising me from spiritual death to spiritual life. I ask that You keep me in good standing with You so that I will be ready to go to heaven as Jesus did. In Jesus' name, I pray, Amen.

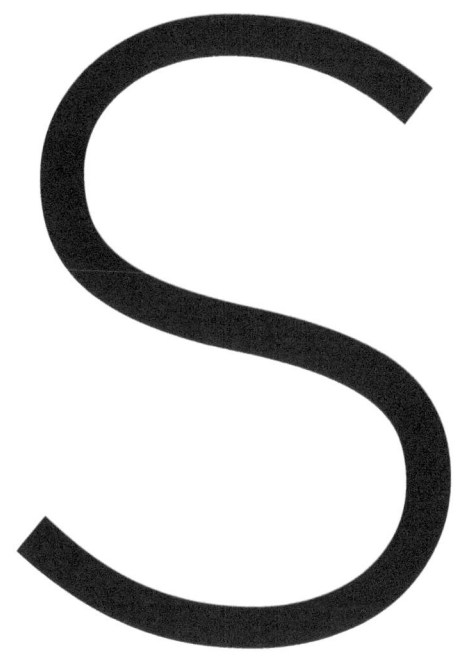

SACRIFICE

to offer something of value to a higher power for the sake of gaining something considered to have higher value.

SCRIPTURES

Offer the sacrifice of righteousness, and put your trust in the LORD.

PSALMS 4:5

The sacrifices of God are a broken spirit, a broken and a contrite heart—these O God You will not despise.

PSALMS 51:17

I will offer to you the sacrifice of thanksgiving, and will call upon the name of the LORD.

PSALM 116:17

I beseech you therefore, brethren, by the mercies of God, that you present your bodies a living sacrifice, holy, acceptable to God, which is your reasonable service.

ROMANS 12:1

HOW THE SCRIPTURES APPLY TO ME

God sacrificed the very best He had for us, His Son, Jesus; Jesus sacrificed the very best He had for us, His life; He asks in return that we offer back sacrifices of repentance for our sins, righteousness, thanksgiving, and our very bodies, for the blessings He has in store for us.

PRAYER

Thank You, heavenly Father and Lord Jesus, for all You have done, for what You are doing, and what You will do in my life and after this life. Let me be a living sacrifice for you. In Jesus' name, I pray. Amen.

TEACH

to impart or enable with knowledge or skill.

SCRIPTURES

Go therefore and make disciples of all nations, baptizing them in the name of the Father and of the Son and of the Holy Spirit, am with you always, even to the end of the age.

MATTHEW 28:19-20

But the Helper, the Holy Spirit, whom the Father will send in My name, He will teach you all things, and bring to your remembrance all things that I said to you.

JOHN 14:26

HOW THE SCRIPTURES APPLY TO ME

God knows that every believer must learn to be fully mature and be most fruitful for Him. Everyone who is a member of the body of Christ needs to be a learner at whatever level they may be. God the Father and Jesus, in their graciousness to us, have made it possible for us always to be learn from Holy Spirit. He dwells within the believer to comfort and teach us and bring all things to our remembrance that we have heard from righteous teachers.

PRAYER

Heavenly Father and Savior Jesus Christ, thank you for sending me a teacher and comforter, the Holy Spirit. Please help me learn to obey the great teacher through His words and works and apply what I've been taught. In Jesus' name, I pray, Amen.

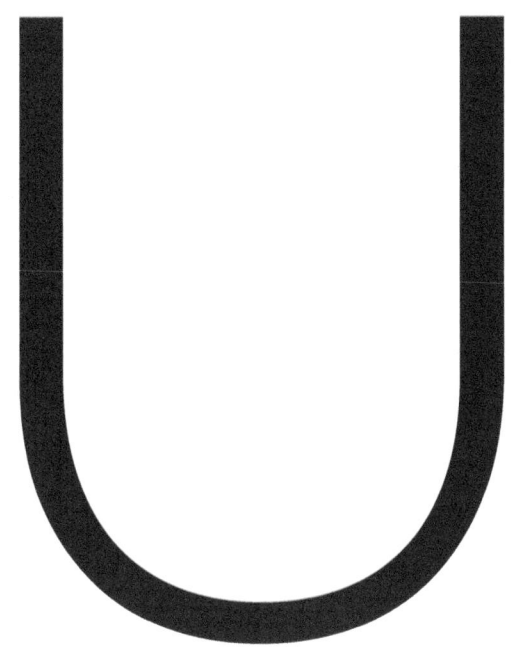

UNDERSTANDING

knowledge of or familiarity with a particular subject or matter.

SCRIPTURES

Give me understanding, and I shall keep Your law; indeed, I shall observe it with my whole heart.
PSALMS 119:34

Trust in the LORD with all your heart, and lean not on your own understanding.
PROVERBS 3:5

Brethren, do not be children in understanding, however, in malice be babes, but in understanding be mature.
1 CORINTHIANS 14:20

And the peace of God, which surpasses all understanding, will guard your hearts and minds through Christ Jesus.
PHILIPPIANS 4:7

HOW THE SCRIPTURES APPLY TO ME

God strongly wants us to learn, know, and understand the truth about Him and His will for us. He says it in many places and in many ways throughout the Scriptures. God does not want us to be ignorant about the importance of a good relationship with Him so that we can reap all of the good benefits He has provided and has in store for us. We need to understand how to please God and not mindlessly follow religious practices like occultists do, which have no meaning as far as God is concerned.

PRAYER

Lord, give me a heart to seek the understanding that is pleasing to You and to know that You are in charge of my life and the course that will keep me doing the things You have me to do for my reward. In Your name, I pray. Amen.

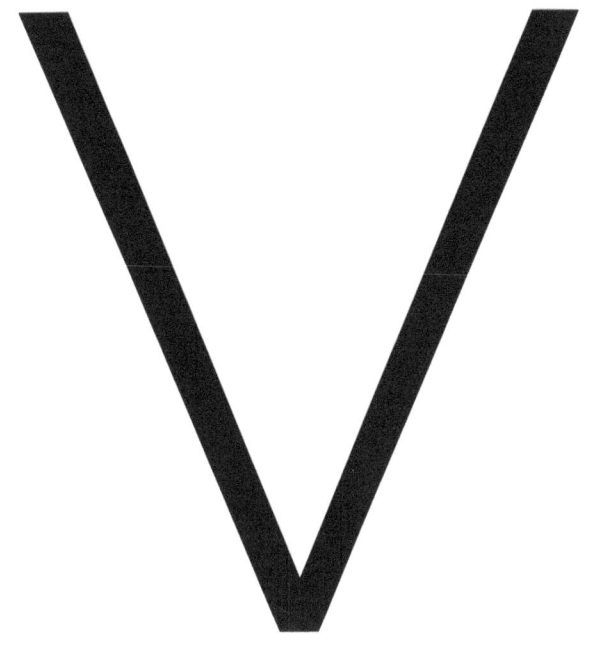

VICTORY

a successful outcome of a struggle against an enemy or against an opposing situation.

SCRIPTURES

But thanks be to God, who gives us the victory through our Lord Jesus Christ.

1 CORINTHIANS 15:57

For whatever is born of God overcomes the world. And this is the victory that has overcome the world—our faith.

1 JOHN 5:4

HOW THE SCRIPTURES APPLY TO ME

God assures us through His written promises in the Scriptures that He has already provided for each of us to come out victorious in whatever the nature of our struggles. To gain victory, all we must do is believe and trust in Him according to His commandments.

PRAYER

Father, Lord God, give me the faith to believe that You are fighting for me and will continue to give me victory over my enemies (Satan's agents). This I pray in Jesus' name. Amen.

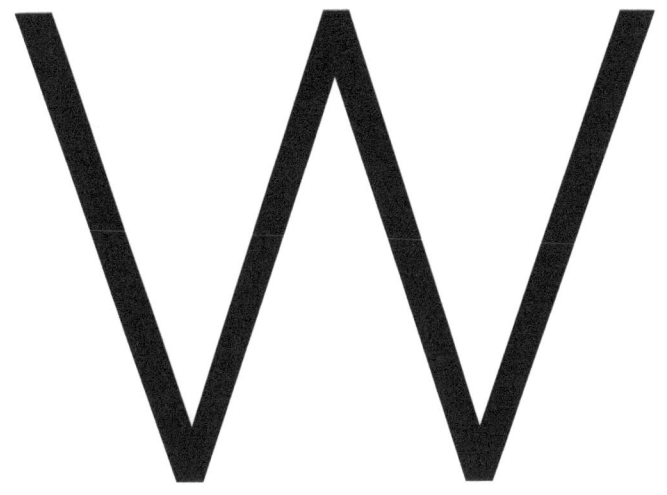

WEAK

lacking in vigor, or strength, or ability.

SCRIPTURES

Watch and pray, lest you enter into temptation. The spirit is indeed willing, but the flesh is weak.
MATTHEW 26:41

I have shown you in every way, by laboring like this, that you must support the weak. And remember the words of the Lord Jesus, that He said, "It is more blessed to give than to receive."
ACTS 20:35

But God has chosen the foolish things of the world to put to shame the wise, and God has chosen the weak things of the world to put to shame the things which are mighty.
1 CORINTHIANS 1:27

HOW THE SCRIPTURES APPLY TO ME

God wants us to realize that although we may be weak in many ways, but if we are in Him, we are still stronger than those of the world in His sight. Thus, we must still be watchful and prayerful and study to be stronger to bear much good fruit for the kingdom of God by faithfully carrying out His assignments.

PRAYER

Father in heaven, thank You for using my weakness to strengthen my life and sending Your Holy Spirit to strengthen me so that I can enjoy Your blessings and bear much fruit for You. I pray in Jesus' name. Amen.

EXALT

holding someone in high regard; to speak highly of someone

SCRIPTURES

Exalt the LORD our God! Bow low before his feet, for he is holy!

PSALM 99:5

Humble yourselves therefore under the mighty hand of God, that he may exalt you in due time.

1 PETER 5:6

HOW THE SCRIPTURES APPLY TO ME

The only way up is down. In our society, everyone is focused on achieving success and so that others may speak well of them. As believers, we are exalted only when we humble ourselves before God and exalt Him. We exalt God by declaring His goodness, speaking well of Who He is and everything He has done.

PRAYER

Heavenly Father, in the name of Jesus, help me to remain humble before you at all times. I declare that You are good, and Your will for my life is perfect. I acknowledge that You are all powerful. You alone hold all wisdom and knowledge. The Earth and everything in it and around it belong to You and You alone. You are God, and there is none greater, mighter, or even in any comparison to you. As I go through my day, remind me to exalt you at every turn. I honor You, Lord. In Jesus' name, I pray. Amen.

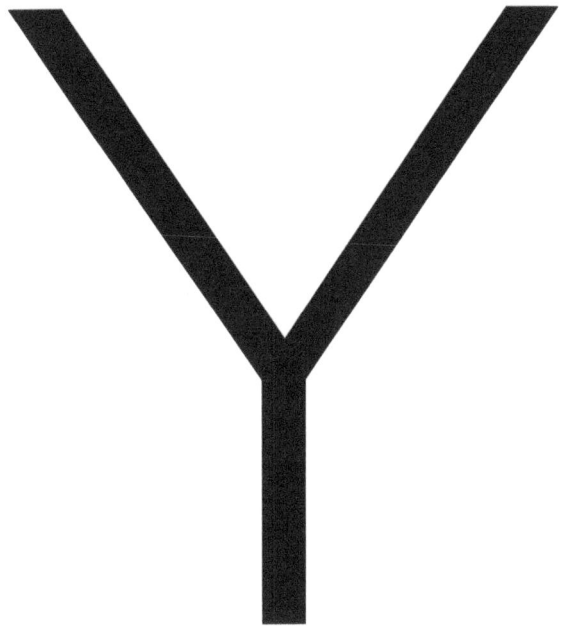

YOKE

a frame for joining together and controlling a pair of plowing animals; symbolic of a device to discipline behavior.

SCRIPTURES

Come to me all who labor and are heavy laden, and I will give you rest. Take My yoke upon you and learn of Me, for I am gentle and lowly in heart, and you will find rest for your souls.

MATTHEW 11:28-29

Stand fast therefore in the liberty by which Christ has made us free, and do not be entangled again with a yoke of bondage.

GALATIANS 5:1

HOW THE SCRIPTURES APPLY TO ME

Jesus is inviting everyone who feels burdened and controlled by the world's agents to take on His discipline of learning about Him. The result will be unlike the world's yoke because Jesus is not like the masters of the world, and the payment will be rest for our souls.

PRAYER

Lord Jesus, I bring my burdens and my fears and lay them down at Your feet. I need Your help because I cannot help myself, and You said Your yoke is easy, which I believe is true; so, in exchange for Your yoke, which I accept, please accept my burdens. I pray this prayer in Your name, Lord Jesus. Amen.

ZION

a term used in reference to Jerusalem, the holy city to be the capital of Israel during the millennium or the time of Christ's reign of earth.

SCRIPTURES

The LORD shall reign forever—You are God, O Zion, to all generations. Praise the LORD!

PSALM 146:10

Let Israel rejoice in their Maker; let the children of Zion be joyful in their King.

PSALMS 149:2

Then I looks, and behold, a Lamb standing in Mount Zion, and with Him one hundred and forty four thousand, having His Father's name written on their foreheads..

REVELATION 14:1

HOW THE SCRIPTURES APPLY TO ME

God is faithful to the promises He made to His people—even during the Old Testament times. However, during this age, He is allowing His Son Jesus to build and prepare His own body, which will assist Him in reigning.

PRAYER

LORD God almighty—You alone are the God over all the kingdoms of the earth. You have made heaven and earth; give ear, O LORD, and hear; listen to all the words of our mouth; deliver us from the hands of our enemies, so that all the kingdoms of the earth will know, O God, that You alone are God.

ALL PRAISES BELONG TO YOU, O GOD! AMEN!

ONE BODY-ONE SPIRIT

There is one body and one spirit, just as you were called in one hope of your calling; one lord, one faith, one baptism; one god and Father of all, who is above all, and through all, and in you all.

EPHESIANS 4:4-6

PRAYER

Father God and Lord Jesus, thank You for helping me understand that by becoming a believer and being baptized in the Holy Spirit, I have become a particular member of Your body, Jesus, by way of Your church. In Your name, I pray. Amen.

2-3

THE POWER OF AGREEMENT

Again I say to you that if two of you agree on earth concerning anything that they ask, it will be done for them by My Father in heaven. For where two or three are gathered together in My name, I am there in the midst of them.

MATTHEW 18:19-20

PRAYER

Lord Jesus, we are indeed grateful for the provision You have made for us to be in righteous agreement with one another in making requests to You. Thank you for Your assurance that what we pray for will be done. Help us who believe and trust in You to learn how to agree in righteousness. Thank You for assuring us that we do not have to be in large crowds to enjoy Your presence. We are encouraged to know that whenever two or three of us believers meet to worship You or make our requests known to You, You are right in our midst. Amen.

FOUR WINDS

And He will send His angels with a great sound of a trumpet, and they will gather together His elect from the **four winds,** *from one end of heaven to the other.*

MATTHEW 24:31

PRAYER

Lord Jesus, who has been given all power in heaven and on earth, I pray that You will help me to live now so that I will be one of Your blessed elects that You will gather from the farthest parts of the earth under heaven when You come in Your glory. Amen!

THE FIFTH COMMANDMENT

Honor your father and your mother that your days may be long upon the land which the LORD your God is giving you.

EXODUS 20:12

PRAYER

Father God, in accordance with Your commandment, as stated in the Old and New Testaments of Your Holy Scriptures, I will be mindful to give honor to all who are due honor, especially to my parents who are alive. I will endeavor to honor their memory as the ones who gave me life to honor and serve You. In Your name, I pray. Amen!

THE SIXTH COMMANDMENT

He said to Him, "Which ones?" Jesus said, "You shall not murder. You shall not commit adultery. You shall not steal. You shall not bear false witness,"

MATTHEW 19:18

PRAYER

Lord Jesus, I am grateful to You for conceiving me, giving me life, and providing for me to have eternal life by giving Your life. Please help me to let Your love prevail in me so that I will always be mindful that You created mankind in Your image for Your glory, and I should work for the salvation of others and refrain from murder in any form, whether in word or deed. Amen.

SEVENTY TIMES SEVEN

Then Peter came to him and asked, "Lord, how often should I forgive someone who sins against me? Seven times?" "No, not seven times," Jesus replied, "but seventy times seven!"

MATTHEW 18:21-22

SCRIPTURES

So watch yourselves! "If another believer sins, rebuke that person; then if there is repentance, forgive. Even if that person wrongs you seven times a day and each time turns again and asks forgiveness, you must forgive."

LUKE 17:3-4

For if you forgive men their trespasses, your heavenly Father will also forgive you. But if you do not forgive men their trespasses, neither will your Father forgive your trespasses.

MATTHEW 6: 14-15

PRAYER

Heavenly Father, in the name of Jesus, teach me by the Holy Spirit how to forgive those who have wronged me, just as I expect to receive forgiveness when I sin against you. Give me the strength to forgive, even when I may be hurting. In Jesus' name, I pray. Amen.

THE EIGHTH COMMANDMENT

You shall not steal.

EXODUS 20:15

Let him that stole steal no longer, but rather let him labor, working with his hands what is good, that he may have something to give to him who has need.

EPHESIANS 4:28

PRAYER

Most Loving Father, thank you for everything you have blessed me with. Thank you for granting me with life, good health, and strength. Thank you for the life and things you have granted to me. By your Holy Spirit, keep me in a place of gratitude. May I always see all that You have done more than I see where I lack. Give me the strength to flee the temptation to take anything that does not belong to me. Help me to walk upright and be integral in all my dealings. In Jesus' name, I pray. Amen.

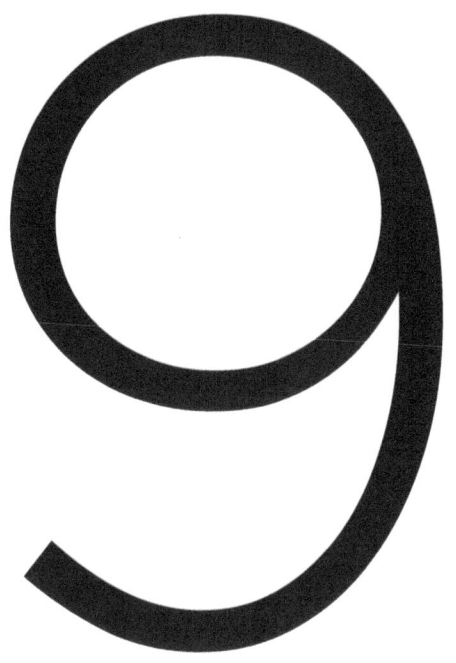

THE NINTH COMMANDMENT

You must not testify falsely against your neighbor.
EXODUS 20:16

A false witness will not go unpunished, and a liar will be destroyed.
PROVERBS 19:9

PRAYER

Heavenly Father, in the name of Jesus, teach me by the Holy Spirit how to speak truth, no matter the consequences I face. Help me understand that lying displeases you. May the words of my mouth and the meditation of my heart be acceptable in your sight. Lord, you are my strength and my redeemer. In Jesus' name, I pray. Amen.

10

TEN PERCENT

One-tenth of the produce of the land, whether grain from the fields or fruit from the trees, belongs to the Lord and must be set apart to him as holy.

LEVITICUS 27:30

SCRIPTURES

"Should people cheat God? Yet you have cheated me!" "But you ask, 'What do you mean? When did we ever cheat you?'" "You have cheated me of the tithes and offerings due to me. You are under a curse, for your whole nation has been cheating me. Bring all the tithes into the storehouse so there will be enough food in my Temple. If you do," says the Lord of Heaven's Armies, "I will open the windows of heaven for you. I will pour out a blessing so great you won't have enough room to take it in! Try it! Put me to the test! Your crops will be abundant, for I will guard them from insects and disease. Your grapes will not fall from the vine before they are ripe," says the Lord of Heaven's Armies.

MALACHI 3:8-11

HOW THE SCRIPTURES APPLY TO ME

God desires us to be cheerful givers. When we give ten percent of the increase God has blessed us with, we honor God and show Him that we trust Him with everything we have. When we give, God promises to ensure we continue to experience his blessings and protection. He even challenges us to put Him to the test!

PRAYER

Heavenly Father, in the name of Jesus, teach me to be a cheerful giver. I experience your blessings every day, and I am so grateful for everything you give. Help me to give as you have instructed us to in Your Word. I give in expectation for blessings so great, I won't have room to receive them. In Jesus' name, I pray. Amen.

May the grace of our lord Jesus Christ be with you all. Amen.

REVELATION 22:21

Acknowledgements

I praise my heavenly Father for loving me, calling me His own, and making me special and a vessel of honor. A woman after His own heart, I will forever be grateful. I give all glory to Him for all the gifts He has given me, and I promise to use them all for His glory. This book is dedicated to God, who gave me the wisdom to write it. Secondly, I dedicate this book to my children.

For his help in providing reviews and essential details related to getting the book completed and published with the quality that is representative of respect for the readers, I would like to thank Dr. Leon Frazier, an ordained teacher of the Word of God, professional educator, and public servant with an extensive record of fruitful service.

About the Author

Janet Hutchful is a native of Nigeria and currently resides in Huntsville, Alabama. A powerful intercessor, prayer warrior, and minister of the Gospel of Jesus Christ, she spends the majority of her day-to-day life helping broken men and women.

Minister Hutchful is a mother of five children and the grandmother of four wonderful grandchildren. Her desire is to be more like Christ as she continues to progress from glory to glory in Him. Teaching the word of God is above all things in her life.

www.ingramcontent.com/pod-product-compliance
Lightning Source LLC
Chambersburg PA
CBHW030446100526
44580CB00001B/2